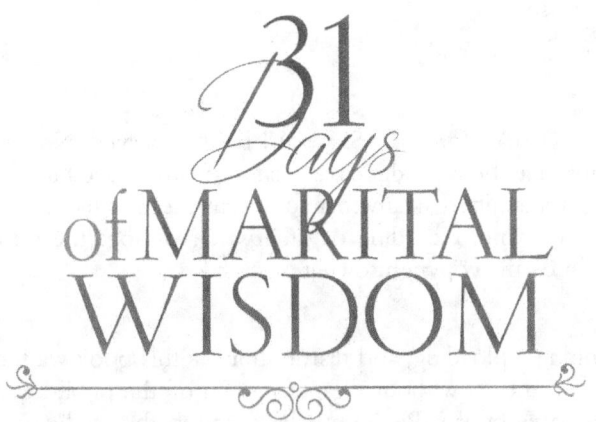

By Jonathan & Sabrina Shaw

JIS Enterprise

Farmingville, New York

Copyright © 2019 Jonathan Shaw. All rights reserved. No part of this publication may be reproduced, stored in or introduced into a retrieval system, or transmitted, in any form or by any means (electronic, mechanical, photocopying, recording or otherwise), without the prior written permission of the copyright owner.

The scanning, uploading, and distribution of this book via the internet or any other means without the permission of the publisher are illegal and punishable by law. Please purchase only authorized electronic editions and do not participate in or encourage electronic piracy of copyright materials. Your support of the author's rights is appreciated.

Limits of Liability ~ Disclaimer

The author and publisher shall not be liable for your misuse of this material. This book is strictly for informational and educational purposes. The purpose of this book is to educate and entertain. The author and publisher do not guarantee that anyone following these techniques, suggestions, tips, ideas, or strategies will become successful. The author and publisher shall have neither liability nor responsibility to anyone concerning any loss or damage caused, or alleged to be caused, directly or indirectly by the information contained in this book.

Cover – Panos Lampridis
Editing – Robin Devonish
Formatting: Chris Papapanagiotou

ISBN 13: 978-0-578-44992-0
Printed in the United States of America

We dedicate this book to our Parents who have shown us what longevity in marriage looks like. Thank You...

Ellis and Tommie Billings, 50 years married

Rudolph and Gwenda Shaw, 51+ years married

PREFACE

It was a sad day in October when my wife's father passed away. We were dating, and I had planned to marry her. While she and her family planned the funeral, she would have moments when she would cry and mourn the passing of her dad. See, she was a daddy's girl. And she had a close relationship with him all her life. Losing him was devastating for her.

One day while at her mom's house, she broke down in tears, while looking at some old photos. I deeply wanted to take the pain away, as most guys want to do. I wondered what I could do to help her. But there was nothing I could do. Grief has to be processed on its own. But one thing I did do... I took her in my arms and simply held her close to me. It was then that I felt her heart beating against my chest. I'm not sure if it was her anxiety of the moment or God making me sensitive to her at that moment. But it seemed as if her heart pounded my chest as I held her. It was then that the Lord spoke to me and said; now I give you One Heart! I was allowed to feel her pain and pray for her as I couldn't before, because now I felt her heart. No words were spoken, simply a merger of two hearts into one.

That's not only the name of the couple's ministry at our church, but it is a prayer that we pray for every couple. We pray that in their marriage they merge as one. A marriage license is the only license you can receive without taking an exam. Besides being of age, there is no governmental assessment that one has to take to be married. Certainly, there are biblical rules and wisdom we could adapt, but it isn't mandated anywhere.

We thought this book of wisdom principles could help marriages as they develop into their merger. Wisdom that some couples didn't receive before the marriage. We want to help every married couple enjoy marital bliss. We certainly don't know it all, but we've gained great insight and have learned wisdom from experiences that allows us to help others.

You have the papers, you have the rings, and you still have the bill from the ceremony. Now gain the wisdom on how to keep this marriage together and alive!

DAY 1

THE ENORMITY OF A MANS FUTURE IS REVEALED IN THE KIND OF WOMAN GOD PUTS BY HIS SIDE.

By Jonathan Shaw

In the book of Genesis, God created the heavens and the earth for five days. On the sixth day, he made the crown of His creation, which is humanity. After God created the man, God noticed something very interesting. The man was not good alone. One would ask a question as to how can the man be alone being that God is there? But God only satisfied the man's spiritual needs and desires. The man lacked human compatibility. This shows us that with everything we have around us; we all need to be around people who are compatible with who we are.

This man is God's prime creation. He is responsible for having dominion over all creation. This man was given the responsibility of managing what God has made. God entrusted the entire world in his hands. This man's well being is God's concern because God has a great investment in him. God cannot and will not just put anyone by his side to satisfy this longing for companionship. So God put the man to sleep, cuts open his side and pulls out a rib and from that rib, God forms a woman. She is someone who is equally powerful, who also has dominion and who has equivalent fellowship with God.

This narrative gives us great insight as to how God thinks about companionship. When God puts someone by your side, it is to secure His investment in you. God will never compromise or threaten His assignment or calling on you by putting you with someone, who at a minimum, doesn't know Him or would cause you to abort His will for you.

In all honesty, the one that God connects you with is a snapshot of what God thinks about you and your future. Brothers, when God puts a good woman by your side, it is because He has great things for you to do and become in your future. Never allow yourself to become intimidated by a well-gifted woman. Her gifts, talents, and abilities are a testament to her greatness. It also reveals what God thinks about you to put her by your side. Remember always to cherish her and honor God for placing her in your life. Subsequently, who you marry is an expression of what you think about yourself. Even worse, it expresses what you think God thinks about you.

NOTES

DAY 2

BEING A BRIDE VS. BEING A WIFE

By Sabrina Shaw

A lot of women dream of having that fairy tale marriage. You know the house with a picket fence, a husband that goes to work in a suit and tie, and those children that are well behaved. Your day starts with preparing breakfast and fixing lunch, kissing everyone and wishing him or her a wonderful day. Then your day resumes with cleaning, doing laundry and cooking. Everyone comes home in a good mood; you're all smiles, everyone is happy, only to start all over again.

That's the scenario of someone who is a wife. I know it entails much more, and I'll get to that, but I'd like to show you a small picture of someone who wants to be married. There are those who go to their own wedding, repeat their vows, and mean some of them. They go to the reception, have a great time, receive gifts and start the next day looking forward to only the honeymoon. This person has no clue that after the honeymoon, real changes are going to happen. All that talk in counseling is about to happen. This person gets home from a wonderful time and doesn't understand that there will be times that you will have to be the first person to get up to get everyone else off on their day's journey.

Are you willing to change your whole lifestyle? And an even deeper question is, are you a wife, to begin with? Of course, your response may be yes. But how prepared are you for that? The scripture says, "He that finds a wife finds a good thing and obtains favor." So you were a wife in waiting. You have been waiting on that day to show how prepared you really are.

Being married is having the papers, man, family, and even fun sometimes, but there are times you don't feel committed to the work of marriage. Being a wife is putting in the work of marriage. Ladies, it's time you take your mind off the wedding day and start putting your efforts into the responsibilities of the marriage, which is being a wife!

NOTES

DAY 3

WHEN YOU REFUSE TO COMMUNICATE WITH YOUR MATE YOU GIVE THEM PERMISSION TO MAKE UP THEIR OWN STORY!

By Jonathan Shaw

If you've been around me for any length of time, you probably have heard me say "The lack of communication is the cancer of all relationships!". This saying is true for all relationships. When we do not communicate with the ones we are in a relationship with, it can be detrimental to the value of it.

The first thing we need to understand is the definition of communication. It is 'understood information conveyed from one party to another.' If it's not understood, it has not been communicated. For years my wife and I have counseled countless couples. The greatest challenges between couples is communication.

In discussions, arguments and debates couples often say things like "I didn't say that" or "where did you get that from?" The amazement that one has when their spouse seems to be making things up is actually their fault. When you do not spend the time to communicate your feelings, your fears and your future to your mate, it leaves them no other option but to make up their mind by developing a story that makes sense to them. This story allows them to be settled with actions and behaviors that have gone un-communicated.

The only way to cancel a made up story or to erase an imaginary picture in your spouse head is to be completely honest when you communicate with them. If not, you've given them the license to film their own movie with you being the star character. Your level of communication chooses whether this is a factual documentary or a fictional drama series.

NOTES

DAY 4

WHO'S WIFE ARE YOU?

By Sabrina Shaw

Get the thought out of your mind that there is only one way to be a wife. What kind of wife does the man you married want or need? Who did he date, and what attributes do you possess that he fell in love with?

Are you funny, do you like people, do you cook, do you clean, and do you have a job? All of these are things he fell in love with. Don't change into someone who he doesn't know.

It's ok to want to change some things if you think it will enhance your marriage. But just because you see other marriages do something, it doesn't mean it will work in your marriage. It is important that you engage in the things that specifically fit for your home, your spouse and your marriage.

Your married friends may have certain things that work for them, but that doesn't mean what works for them will work for you. Some techniques are general; others are private. For instance, some men want a home cook meal every night. Other men don't mind eating leftovers. It is only important to know what your husband wants. And that goes for the men as well. Some women want to see a six-pack. Other women don't mind a little extra cushion on her man.

While you were courting, there were eye-opening situations that caused a red flag to go up. Was it a deal breaker then? Did you say, "I can handle that?" And when it came up in the marriage you did just that; you handled it. Often couples are shocked when they notice something in the marriage that was always there. They just failed to pay attention to it. I guess the statement is true… Love does make you blind!

You must learn each other likes and dislikes, wants, desires and needs to be who the other needs you to be. I mean whose wife are you anyway? Don't start talking about what someone else is doing for her husband or what someone is doing for their wife. What are you doing for yours?

Notes

DAY 5

THE WORST THING YOU COULD EVER DO TO YOUR SPOUSE IS TRY TO MAKE THEM JUST LIKE YOU!

YOU DIDN'T MARRY YOURSELF

By Jonathan Shaw

Remember when you guys first started dating? Remember when you first fell in love with each other? You admired their quirkiness, their weird way of doing things and their awkward style. You thought it was the cutest thing.

At one point you were attracted to their difference. Somehow over time, their difference began to annoy you to the point of trying to change them and firmly suggesting your spouse do things the way you do and think the way you think. This is the worst thing you could ever do to your mate! It is our difference that makes us great not our similarities! You have always been different people to each other. Don't try to change that now. Learn to embrace and celebrate your differences. Ultimately, you must look at things in realms of the outcome. Does the job get done? It doesn't matter if he does it this way or she does it that way, as long as it gets done, and it doesn't hurt the unit. You may do things differently, but as a unit, you both need to think in the interest of the unit and not personal validation.

People work overtime trying to turn their mate into themselves. Today is a good day to admit that your spouse is different from you. In the notes section for today, I want you to write the difference you have with your mate. And then write ways that you can celebrate and embrace these differences. It will remind you of why you feel in love in the first place.

Notes

DAY 6

JUGGLERS

BUDGET YOUR TIME OR YOU'LL JUGGLE YOUR PRIORITIES.

By Sabrina Shaw

I know we are all busy doing so much. Life can become so overwhelming that you can lose track of time with all you have to do. You ever lie down at night, exhausted from the day, but still fill unfulfilled because you still have so many things on your agenda to take care of? That's life!

In marriage, we have to learn to juggle our time. We must be excellent time managers. We have to pay close attention to what we are doing with our time that our priorities don't go lacking. That means we must balance priorities. To everything, there is a season, a time. I know most people want to be spontaneous, but something gets lost in spontaneity. It can be something small, but it was still a priority.

In marriage, you have to tend to the children, the bills, the church, the business, your spouse, God and most times forget about yourself. To meet all these obligations, we have to learn to budget our time better. Where you spend time is what's working. If you don't spend quality time in that area, it will lack.

Your husband/wife is your priority, so budget your time in the day to ensure your priorities are met with your mate. Many spouses often feel left out because the attention has gone to other things. It's known of couples who grow old together sometimes get a divorce because once all the kids are gone, retirement has begun and the house is quiet; they don't know each other. All the while they were building a life they forgot to live with each other. Make sure this doesn't happen in your marriage. Be a great time manager.

NOTES

DAY 7

MEN, JUST BECAUSE YOU'VE GOT HER DOESN'T MEAN YOU HAVE HER.

By Jonathan Shaw

When we first start dating, we all LIE!!! The women lie by beating their face with make-up, forming their bodies with contour undergarments, weaving their hair with the latest bundle of hair and shoving their feet in the highest of heels. The men lie by clearing out their bank accounts for an evening of fine dining, taking long showers and the closest shaves. They get haircuts and clean the car real good to give a good impression. IT'S ALL LIES!!! It wouldn't be so bad if each of them didn't appear like they live like that or look that way all the time. But it's just a façade.

Both ladies and gentlemen must realize that what you do to get them, you must continue to keep them. Otherwise, they will eventually see the "real" you!

Men, you especially have to know that just because you 'got her' don't mean you 'have her.' It's possible for women to be with you but not feel connected to you. A good woman will do her best to love you and try her best to win your love. But, if you don't continue to keep interest in her and the things that interest her, she will not be there even though she is physically there.

Men sometimes work overtime to gain a woman's interest and love to only lose it by not keeping to their unspoken promises, or even worse, un-communicated expectations. Men create expectations by habits. If you begin with flowers and candy, you have to keep it up. If you begin with phone calls and pet names, you have to continue doing that. These things create expectations that the woman wants you to keep up. A failure to do so will result in her being disappointed in the relationship. You may have her, but you lost her, even though she's still there.

Notes

WHOSE CYCLE IS IT ANYWAY?
By Sabrina Shaw

Learn his cycles so you'll be right on time.

Ladies, have you ever wanted to ask your husband a difficult question, but you weren't sure if it was a good time to ask? How about this, you see something wrong, and wanting to ask the question "What's wrong?". You think you're being sensitive, but he doesn't want you asking anything. He's not in the mood.

Men often say that the worst thing they can hear from their wife is "can we talk?". These can be dreadful words. But if you catch him in the right mood, you may get a better response.

There is a certain time to ask. Men have cycles too. For some men, certain questions they don't like period. You would think asking what's wrong is a sign that you're paying attention, that something has happened and he's not himself. Some of you ask, and when his response is a flip one, you then give your flip response, and the situation has gone downhill. But you must understand that men rationalize situations differently than women. Men tend to internalize while women are very expressive. But sometimes the reverse is also true. Women, you must learn that just because you want to say it, doesn't mean it's a good time to say it. Learn his cycles!

Listen when something is bothering you, sometimes you don't want to talk either. You can avoid an argument if you analyze the mood. When the mood gets better, and then with a sensitive voice, asks the hard question. More than likely, you will get a decent response. I think this also helps when you're trying for a pair of shoes, or a bag too. LOL

But seriously, there are going to be times when you have to understand his cycle. When you do, you will say what needs to be said, but, when it needs to be said.

NOTES

DAY 9

YOU CAN'T HAVE A SUCCESSFUL MARRIAGE IF YOUR MONEY IS DIVORCED.

By Jonathan Shaw

The top three reasons marriages end in divorce are infidelity, sex, and MONEY! Marriage is not only a divine covenant between a man and a woman, but it's also a business merger between two corporations. Married couples must have the very difficult discussion of merging their monies. When you come from being single and living single, you must physically, mentally, emotionally and financially adjust yourself. YOU ARE NO LONGER SINGLE!

Too often married couples are living like roommates. They split everything, including the bills. This is a travesty waiting to happen. When you get married, you are marrying the entire person. You marry their family, their fears, their faults, and their finances. It's all yours too!

I recommend that every couple sit to a table and do a full workout of their finances. This has to be a very transparent conversation. It is also a good idea to get a certified financial planner involved in the process so you can create a plan for your future together.

Here are a few suggestions as a first step to merging these companies. Every married couple should have four bank accounts. 1) A combined checking account 2) A combined savings account 3) His personal account 4) Her personal account. From the combined accounts you should take care of the entire house bills and expenses for the children. Who makes more money should be immaterial. All the money should be directly deposited into the combined checking account. Then a portion should be placed into your savings account. No monies should be touched from the savings unless you both agree. With the personal accounts, you can do whatever you like.

Another great rule to employ is what I call the $500 rule! But it can be whatever you both agree upon. The $500 rule says that you cannot spend more than $500 without your spouse consent and approval.

If you use these small suggestions, you will properly merge these companies, and it can be a smooth transition. Your marriage will never be truly successful if your money is still acting single.

NOTES

DAY 10

YOU MUST CHANGE, YOU'RE MARRIED NOW.
By Sabrina Shaw

S ingle? NOT!

Let's face it. You have found it difficult to change from single to married. In singleness, you're so used to doing things by yourself, and for yourself that you have to adjust your entire life to a married mindset.

I know what that's like; I was one who was so independent that I forgot a man was in the house. When things needed to be done, I would do it without asking for help. Why, because I could, and I did. But you've got to get to the place of a different mindset. You're not by yourself anymore. Of course, things are going to be different, there's testosterone in the house, and they don't do things like you do things. Everyone is there to meet the needs of each other. Everything that happens now may require a conversation, a forethought and an approval. What do I mean by approval? You shouldn't or can't do things because you think you should or even if you can. Your decision and choices aren't just yours anymore. You're married now!!!! You have to start saying things like "Babe would you mind if…" It is not a hard question when you've changed your mindset.

Are you single? NOT! Some people aren't married because they couldn't get married. The issue is that they are too selfish to get married. Marriage requires compromise and meeting the needs of others more than you. Selfish people don't want to do that. Singleness fosters the mindset of individuality and selfishness. When you get married, you discard that mindset and adopt a new mindset of marriage.

NOTES

Day 11

SEX HAPPENS 10% OF THE TIME BUT HAS 100% OF IMPORTANCE!

By Jonathan Shaw

The Bible says that marriage is honorable and the bed is undefiled (Hebrews 13:4). The marital bed is a consecrated place. It is a sacred bond of intimacy that only husband and wives should share. Because sex has this much power, it is easy to be misused or abused.

Unfortunately, some women use sex as a tool of manipulation, which is, a very dangerous game to play. It is also a demonstration of witchcraft tendencies. The Bible teaches that manipulation is as of witchcraft. Never withhold sex from your husband because you have a problem with him. In reverse, men you must understand that sex to the woman is an act of unity and personal intimacy. If she feels unloved, unsupported or unattractive, performing sex as a chore cheapens the experience to her. If you want a pleasurable time with her, make sure she's emotionally comfortable to do so.

Sex is the natural satisfaction that we get from our mates; similar to the spiritual satisfaction we get from God. God does not satisfy our natural desires, but He gives us a person who will, our spouse! This furthers the point that our sexual interaction should be with one person. When you invite other people into your bedchambers, you are becoming sexually polytheistic. It is like serving two or more gods.

Women, your body belongs to your husband, and it is meant to serve his needs. The same in reverse; husbands, your body belongs to your wife, and it is meant to serve her needs. I'm sure most men won't have a problem with that.

These personal and intimate behaviors occur about 10% of the time in a marriage… unless you guys go at it all the time. I hope that yall come up for air. But, the importance of a sexual encounter is extremely crucial. Make sure your spouse is sexually satisfied. Now, remember, this is only for "MARRIED" COUPLES!

NOTES

Day 12

SUBMISSION GOES BOTH WAYS!
By Sabrina Shaw

Let's begin this with scripture, Ephesians 5:21-22. "Submitting yourselves one to another in fear of the Lord."

Now you knew there was going to be submission in your marriage. People don't know many verses in the Bible, but most people know submission is there. When the preacher asks the question will you love, honor, and obey, you knew there was submission in there. The question is, did you take it seriously?

Submission doesn't mean slavery! It is a combination of two words. The prefix SUB means to come under. The suffix mission means a goal or purpose. So submission is coming under the goal or purpose. That is not only the duty of the wife, but also that is the duty of both parties in the marriage. The husband must submit as well.

Ok, what does it mean to submit to my husband? When there are those hard decisions, decisions for our family, he has the last word. And do you know what submission to one another is; he asks me my opinion before he even makes the decision. God didn't expect me to leave my brain at the altar when I got married. Submission doesn't mean you don't have an opinion. Submission is not a sign that you're weak; it's not a sign that you should be talked down to. I would say submission is a sign of strength and respect that you have for one another. This will help you live a content and peaceful life.

So stop avoiding the need for submission in the marriage and submit to each other about your home, family, housework, business, and ministry.

NOTES

DAY 13

IF YOU HAVEN'T LEARNED YOUR MATES RHYTHM, YOU WILL BE OFF BEAT TO THEIR FLOW.

By Jonathan Shaw

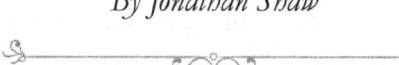

When I was about ten years old, my parents sent me to music lessons to learn to play the drums. I was excited because I thought that I would be playing like a professional drummer by the first lesson. I had new drumsticks, and the music I wanted to play.

Well, to my surprise when I went to the lesson, the first class was talking about the different parts of the drums. That was boring to say the least. I wanted to hit something. Weeks later, I finally got a chance to play the drums. My music instructor took out the snare drum and sat me in front of it. I was like, where are the other pieces? He put a drum book in front of me and instructed me to hit the snare while holding the sticks a certain way (the correct way). The book was just a bunch of L's & R's. I was like what is that? He said its LEFT & RIGHT. I learned to play the drums by hitting LEFT, RIGHT, LEFT – LEFT, RIGHT – RIGHT! While I desired to be the next professional drummer, my music instructor was trying to teach me rhythm.

Amazingly, that is the same challenge in marriages. Many want to jump in bed and be the next super porn star to their mate, but never take the time to learn their rhythm. Every person has a sexual rhythm. Some may be fast while others rhythm is slow. But if your goal is to please yourself only, you will ruin the rhythm of your marriage.

Wife, it is important to know when your husband's rhythm is. You have to study his patterns. When he looks at you a certain way, you must know what that means. You have to know if he's an early morning lover or does he have an evening flame. Sometimes it's both!

Husbands, you must study her rhythm as well. Like most women, she may have a high libido right before her menstrual. Or that may be the time that she doesn't want you to touch her. When engaging in sex, she may want more caressing and foreplay when you want to hit the gas and get to it. Learn her rhythm, and you will always get to where you want to go. And the journey there will be enjoyable for both of you.

NOTES

DAY 14

PUT GOD FIRST!

By Sabrina Shaw

Now, this should be the first thing to talk about because God has to be the one in front of, on the side of, and all around a marriage. After all, we get married in the sight of God and witnesses. I'm not sure if most couples realize, when they got married, four persons were actually at the altar... It was the bride, the groom, the preacher, and GOD!

I know many couples are getting married these days that don't connect to the traditional Christian marriage culture. But to us as believers in Jesus Christ, this union is a sacred one, and God created the institution of marriage. Therefore we believe that God still honors the marriage covenant the way He intended it to be. A marriage is a picture of Christ relationship with the church, which is the image of God. Putting God first is the only way to do it correctly.

While we believe in marital counseling, we also believe that couples should pray for their marriage. Who are you going to pray to when you don't know what to do? God, what am I going to do? When dealing with your spouse, and there is a major difference of opinion in the home. You'll never pray so much until you get married. Those things that you try to talk about with your mate that seem to never change, talk to God. Since God is the creator of marriage and the creator of your mate, He knows exactly how to handle the situation. My husband always told me the only time you can change a man, is when he's in diapers. And this is true. If God won't change him, neither will you.

You will not make it in a marriage without God.

NOTES

DAY 15

YOU CAN'T MASTER MARRIAGE UNTIL YOU'VE MASTERED SINGLENESS.

By Jonathan Shaw

Marriage is a beautiful bond shared between husband and wife. It is when a man and a woman find their counterpart and consent to spend the rest of their lives together. The bliss of marriage is filled with pleasures untold, peace unspoken and limitless joy. When two people find each other and are joined together in this sacred union, it is like heaven on earth.

But the truth is you cannot enjoy all of this until you first enjoy YOU! Your singleness is a vital step in your marriage. Many of the bad habits you pick up in singleness you bring into a marriage. If marriage is your goal for a relationship, you must begin to make adjustments now to your personality and character to suit a lifelong relationship.

During your time as a single individual, you need to begin to understand who you are as a person. You need to know your likes, dislikes, desires, and buttons. This is going to be key in a marriage. Learn to master you. If you don't know who you are, you will never be able to make anyone else happy. You will make the grave mistake that far too many people have made; which is to try to discover happiness through another individual. This is not only wrong it is unfair to anyone.

It is unfair to put the pressure of your happiness on another individual, including your spouse.

Your happiness and joy is your discovery and responsibility. Understanding this will make you fulfilled and complete to be the perfect spouse for your mate. When you are whole, you present a whole person to the relationship. One of the biggest misconceptions ever told is that a marriage is 50/50. Not true! Marriage is 100/100! It is when a whole complete man connects with a whole complete woman.

Too often people only come to the relationship with only 50%, and they wonder why they aren't 100% satisfied. You shouldn't get rid of all your friends, neither should the guy stop having a boys night out. Those things are healthy in a marriage. Time apart makes the coming together much more potent. Only end the relationships with the individuals who don't respect your responsibility as a husband/wife.

DAY 16

LIVING WITHOUT HIM?

By Sabrina Shaw

In today's society, married people are getting divorced for the craziest things. The simplest things have become deal breakers. He leaves the toilet seat up ALL THE TIME; He doesn't help clean, etc. These are things you could have discussed beforehand. But let me ask you this, can you live without him? How seriously did you take, "Till death do us part."

There are other things more serious than those tedious things. You must learn to handle sickness and in health. He's sick… will you stay? How about if he needs a caretaker… will you do it? How long are you willing to have patience through all of this? Will you believe God with him and for him? Are you in it so deep that if you have to wipe his nose, clean him, change him… Are you all in? His trials will test your faithfulness and your love.

I've watched my mom after my father passed away, and she recalls his death more than a little bit. She may not remember everything, but she remembers she was married 50 years. I've asked how they did it. There was a balance in their relationship and communication that only they understood. I see her living, but her living without him, of course, has changed. Are you married to the one that you can't live without?

Can you live without him? What drew you to him, that would get you to stay, and what would make you walk away?

I want to grow old with mine. And I know that if he has to take care of me, he would. I certainly will take care of him. Do you have that?

Notes

DAY 17

YOUR MARRIAGE IS THE IMAGE OF GOD AND THE PICTURE OF CHRIST & HIS CHURCH.

By Jonathan Shaw

The Bible says husbands love your wives even as Christ loved the church and gave himself for it (Ephesians 5:25). This is a picture of perfect love. God often uses symbolism to point to something more meaningful. He used a lamb to point to Jesus; He used materials and furniture to represent His presence and other sacred things. The same is for the marital covenant. The picture of a husband and wife is the picture of Christ and the church. When you look at this parallel, you will see a beautiful picture of a perfect relationship. Let's take a look:

CHRIST	CHURCH	HUSBAND	WIFE
Head	Body	Head	Family
Vine	Branches	Giver	Receiver
High Priest	Royal Priesthood	High Priest	Priest
Bridegroom	Bride	Groom	Bride

This is a great model of the roles played in marriage. If every husband studied Christ and His attributes and determined to become that, it would make the marriage perfect. In the same respect, if the wife would study and obtain the true attributes of the church, she would biblically fulfill her role in the marriage.

Also, not only is the marital unit a picture of Christ and the church, but it is also a picture of God. Now, please understand that God is a Spirit. But Genesis 1 says that He created mankind in His image. He created them male and female, which is the image of God! God has no gender, but we use male pronouns to describe Him because of His paternal nature. The image of God is a man and a woman, which is marriage. So it is important for each couple to know that your marriage is telling the world, this is what God looks like. What image is your marriage presenting to the world?

NOTES

SET A DATE FOR A DATE!
By Sabrina Shaw

Do you guys remember when you first met? You went on dates, vacations, and outings all the time. You would be spontaneous and get up and go. Unfortunately, couples allow that to die when they get married. They allow life, children, and jobs to take over their dating time. But my advice to you is… Don't stop enjoying one another!!!

Who said after the wedding you can't date? LOL. You must date each other. Don't stop having fun. Dinner, picnics, vacations, do it all. What do the two of you enjoy doing? Do that! Going to the movies, bowling, roller-skating or just a walk in the park, you have to agree to have fun together again.

My husband and I after one year of marriage didn't have much money, so we had to improvise. We got a blanket, made sandwiches; a bottle of sparkling cider, and sat in the middle of the floor listening to music. And by the way, it wasn't gospel. It was Barry White and Jazz. Listen, we like each other. Only people who don't like each other don't spend time together.

Dress up, smell good; look good. Get your hair done, nails done and lashes. Girl please, Saturday's aren't look jacked up day. You can still do your thing. Tell yourself 'I'm an all year round good-looking woman.'

Women aren't the only ones with the responsibility, you husbands must dates your wives again. When you first met her, you pulled out the stops to impress her. She got flowers, went to dinner, you pulled out the chair and complimented her all the time. You would even shave, shower and wear cologne. When you got married, it all stopped. Brothers, you have to do what you did to get her, to keep her.

It's about time for a good date, don't you think!

NOTES

DAY 19

WHEN YOU REMOVE THE SYMBOL OF YOUR MARRIAGE, YOU GIVE YOURSELF PERMISSION TO ACT LIKE YOU'RE NOT.

By Jonathan Shaw

In our western world, we have many things that we use to symbolize a marital covenant. Through the many different ceremonies I've performed, I have seen it all. Couples have chosen to wear the traditional rings. I have seen them plain and simple, blinged out in diamonds, different metals, or simply significant to the bride and groom. I have also witnessed, tattooed rings, neck chains, bracelets and many other significant expressions of their marital covenant. No matter what they choose, it all means something to them.

More traditionally, the bride and groom puts a ring on the left hand, ring finger to signify their union. This finger has emotional significance and anatomical significance as well. This is the only finger on the body that has a direct artery to the heart. Whoever places a ring on this finger is supposed to be the only one that has a direct line to your heart.

While this offers us a romantic fairytale of a story, people have chosen to use many symbols. Whatever symbol you decide to use for your covenant, it should be honored and maintained. Husbands and wives have been known to lose their rings because they take them off for many reasons. I know some of you are going to use the excuse that it got too tight, or, you work with your hands and you don't want to mess up your ring and my favorite, you are not a jewelry person. LOL

Whatever excuse you use, when you remove your marital symbol you immediately permit yourself to act like you're not married. It's like saying "I'm released from prison" or "I'm free" or even worse "I'm available". If that symbol is what you both decided upon to use to represent that you are married, you should keep it on. It is the statement to the world that you're taken. Surely, your marriage is deeper and more significant than a mere ring, but if that ring is an announcement to the world that you are married, then you shouldn't be silent about it.

Notes

DAY 20

SUPPORT HIM... DREAMS DO COME TRUE!
By Sabrina Shaw

It's a sad day when you can't support your man. Now I'm not talking about him staying home and you at work, and while he's home, he does nothing. No, ma'am! Some men have dreams and aspirations, just like you have dreams and aspirations. Some things in their life couldn't and didn't come true until you came along Mrs. Help Meet.

Let me share my personal story with you. When I dated my husband, I knew there was something special about him. First and foremost, I knew he was anointed and was a leader in his own right. To me, he was and is one of the greatest preachers out there. One night, the Lord showed me who my husband was. Now, we did speak about him Pastoring, but that night it was right in my face. I wanted to talk about what I believe God shared with me concerning him, but my husband said he couldn't talk about it now. I had to respect his wishes. Remember the previous nugget about learning his cycle?

After three days, he shared with me God's plan for him. You would think after God already shared with me what He was doing with my hubby, I wouldn't be shocked. However, I was. I hadn't let what God showed me to soak in. Why not? You may ask. Because it didn't just concern him but me too. There were going to be changes and lots of them. What in the world happens next?

He was already itinerate, so did this mean he's going to be gone a lot, and up late? Am I going to lose my time with him? But I had to understand. This is his passion. It's what he loves and does well. But most of all, this is what he is called to do. Well, when I thought 'Oh, this is going to be ok, he's working, and I'm working, at least we have money coming in.' Huh, the Lord threw a monkey wrench in that. Well, we started our church, Crown Ministries with just five people, and you know he couldn't get a salary. Then my hubby was laid off, and the preaching engagements weren't pouring in. I'm the only one working, but I know there's a plan, and that plan includes me supporting my husband. Those were some very trying years. We suffered many things. Lights were turned off, cars repossessed, rent was due, were just a few of the problems we faced. But I stuck it out with him.

It's 16 years later, and can I say it is well worth it. Now Dr. Shaw has several companies that he owns besides doing ministry. He even allowed me to resign from my job to be the housewife that I always wanted to be. I supported him with his calling and dream then, and now he takes pleasure in supporting me. Ladies, support him, believe in him and pray for him. It's going to turn around eventually.

NOTES

DAY 21

INFIDELITY HAPPENS WAY BEFORE SEX.

By Jonathan Shaw

In my opinion, there are many scary scriptures in the Bible. One of which is Matthew 5:28 which says "But I say unto you, that whosoever looks on a woman to lust after her hath committed adultery with her already in his heart." Like WHOOOAAA!!!!

You mean to tell me that if I even look at a woman the wrong way, I have already committed adultery. If that's the case, many of us are guiltier than we think. That's because God knows something that we don't. Infidelity happens way before you get to the bedroom. Something occurs in the heart and mind.

It is important that you keep certain doors closed and don't entertain certain ideas. Especially when those ideas can foster an appetite that only your mate should satisfy. Flirting, being overly nice, paying extra attention to someone are all gestures that could lead to other things. Now I'm not saying you can't be a nice individual, but you have to know yourself enough to know how much is too much and how long is too long.

I want to explore for a moment the mind of those who allow their minds to wander outside their marriage. While it is wrong to cheat and a sin to abandon your covenant without agreement, why does one want to entertain other options? Is it to say they're bored, unwelcomed, don't feel it or are they just greedy and nasty?

There are many questions as to why one would step out of the confines of the marital covenant. But while most couples get stuck in the what (sex), they never explore the why (mindset). The truth is they were cheating way before the first kiss of the other person.

NOTES

DAY 22

ALL IS FAIR IN LOVE AND WAR!

By Sabrina Shaw

Who said because you're married, you won't disagree? In a marriage, you're not going to have one fight; you're going to have many. No one is perfect. You know that each of you have your own opinion, and won't agree on everything, right? The problem is we get mad when the other doesn't conform to our way of thinking.

I think a lot of us hold our feelings in. We keep them to ourselves so that we don't have the task of feeling uncomfortable talking about it. But does it feel better holding it in and getting over it, or talking about it and getting over it? I've tried both of these methods, and I guess I can say talking about it helps because you get to hear the mind of the other. But you will not always feel better, and still may not understand. But there's knowledge of what you didn't know before that comes from a conversation. Why do they feel that way; what happened; what did you or they do to prompt this feeling? All of this comes of a good conversation.

Just like knowing their cycle, you know what words will take them there. You know what buttons to push. Do you intend to push the button on purpose because you're mad? Because when you say too much, other unintended things come out. You start calling each other names and begin to say things you know will hurt. That's hitting below the belt. Say what you mean, mean what you say. It may still hurt, but the issue still needs to be addressed. Unnecessary comments aren't needed. You can fight, but fight fair. Listen to each other… don't be the only one talking. Does he hear you, is he listening to you? And the same thing goes for you. Are you looking out for each other's best interest? If these are not the concerns, then you are fighting for no reason. You're going to fight, but fight fair and fight with a purpose.

NOTES

Day 23

ALWAYS REMAIN A STUDENT OF YOUR MATE. YOU'RE PART OF THE REASON WHY THEY'VE CHANGED.

By Jonathan Shaw

According to physiological identity theory, a human being evolves every seven years. Within every seven years, major events occur in someone's life that causes that person to see life differently. A life, a death, a new job, purchase or loss of a home, a marriage, etc., are all major life events that causes a person to evolve. Therefore, in a marriage, your mate is changing at least every seven years.

This would then mean that the person you married 20 years ago is not the same person you are married to today. They have changed at least twice and are on their way to another change. This can be challenging for you because it seems like you've been spending all your time to learn them, and then they change on you.

These factors can only mean one thing. You have to remain a student of your mate. You must study them at all times. Discover new things about your mate that you never knew before. Couples married for 50 years or more have been shocked at the new things they've discovered. The truth is that there isn't anything new to learn, their spouse simply evolved as a person and are now doing new things that they have never done before.

The irony of it all is while you may be frustrated by learning all the new things about your mate; you have been the greatest contributor to their evolution. A person evolves most in marriage — all the more reasons why you must remain committed to being in the class of YOUR SPOUSE. You must learn their ways, their habits, and their verbal and non-verbal communication. The moment you drop out of school is the moment you fail at the relationship.

NOTES

DAY 24

TOUCH ME IN THE MORNING
By Sabrina Shaw

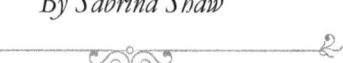

Why do some people use their time of intimacy as a weapon? I know you are attracted to one another right? You must be ready, willing and able to be intimate with your spouse. Ok, I know after the fight, or disagreement, no one wants to get intimate. Well, he may want to!

On the other hand, after a fight, someone wants that closeness in hopes that things will feel better. You've probably said, 'I don't want him to touch me after that.' There are times when neither of you will want to touch each other. But I must be honest, making up is fun.

Don't forget the love you have for one another which shouldn't die because of bad blood. Let's flip this for a moment, what happens when the touching stops or when he's trying to cuddle doesn't happen as often? You'll miss it.

Oh, if he wants it all the time. You better be Ready, Willing, and you know you're Able. It could be 10:00 p.m., 2:00 a.m., before work, after work. Whenever, wherever shouldn't matter. The saying is true; you don't want his eyes wandering or his feelings wandering because he's not getting it at home. How about you make him tired, too tired to go anywhere else. Don't use sex as a weapon to destroy, rather use it as a tool to build. You'll enjoy the process!

Notes

IT'S INEVITABLE THAT YOU'LL FIGHT, SO LEARN TO FIGHT FAIR.

By Jonathan Shaw

I love to hear the stories of engaged couples or newlyweds that they don't ever want to fight. They go on and on about their love for each other and how they work things out and never argue.

This is the case until they get good into the marriage and the first big disagreement comes up. Then the boxing gloves come on... or off! To many couples surprise, the person that they fell madly in love with can also be the person they hate the most. The dichotomy of marriage is that you can love them and dislike them all at the same time. Fighting is inevitable!

You guys are going to fight! You might as well get that in your head. Fighting in marriage will happen just like jumping into a pool of water, you will get wet. It's going to happen. Since fighting is a reality, then all couples must learn to fight fair. Just as if you jumped in that pool, you must learn to swim. You must know the rules in fighting in marriage.

Just as there are rules in boxing, so are there rules in fighting in marriage. It's not a street fight... neither is your mate your archenemy, even though they feel like it at the moment. Knowing the rules of fighting in a marriage can save the marriage from unnecessary future damage. Couples tend to say things and even do things during fighting that they regret later. Tension rises, emotions flare and then an explosion happens. There are ways to prevent these calamities.

Some of the rules in fighting in a marriage are: First, don't do or say anything disrespectful. Second, no hitting below the belt. Third, choose your words carefully. Be sure to say what you mean and mean what you say. Fourth, stick to the fight until you come to a resolution. Your marriage isn't based upon love; it's based upon commitment. You must even commit to the fight.

So put your gloves back on, go to your separate corners and wait for the bell. When you hear the bell, come out swinging!!!

NOTES

DAY 26

TWO ARE BETTER THAN ONE!
By Sabrina Shaw

The Bible speaks in Ecclesiastes 4:9, "Two are better than one…" Couples must learn to power up together. Power up – Partner together with a common goal to be happy. Where there is unity, there is strength. The truth is, we are strong by ourselves, but the strength of a strong union can go a long way. Some attacks can be defeated when you have a mate that has the strength you may not have.

One of my greatest joys of marriage is doing ministry with my husband. We are a power couple together. Now I must be honest; I never had a desire to be in ministry. I always told my husband that ministry is what you do. I'll sit back and support you. But he wouldn't have it. He compelled me to join him in ministry, and I'm glad he did.

I enjoy changing people's lives with him. I used to joke with my husband and tell him, that he doesn't come with me to work and help me at my job, why do I have to go to work with him and help at his job. The truth is, we are better together. In his own right my husband is, hands down, flatfooted, an awesome preacher. He can easily hold his own. And the Lord has been gracious to me to give me a gift to sing. People often express to me how blessed they are when I minister in song (to God be the Glory). We both can stand on our own with our gifts, but when you put the two together…

EXPLOSIVE!!!

The scripture also says in Deuteronomy 32:30 "One can chase a thousand, and two put ten thousand." Because two are better than one! You are better together. Combine your efforts, your gifts, and your vision, and you'll see something spectacular. Why do it alone when your powers together cannot be defeated.

NOTES

DAY 27

YOU MUST GIVE THE SAME ADVANTAGES, OPPORTUNITIES, AND GRACE YOU WANT FOR YOURSELF.

By Jonathan Shaw

One of the challenges in a marriage is the willingness to be fair! We often view situations from a selfish perspective. We become self-serving when it comes to defending ourselves or even proving our case. This is not only unfair, but it can become an enemy to longevity in any relationship.

We often allow ourselves graces and forgiveness that we don't offer to others. We allow ourselves to get away with murder while we won't allow our mates to commit a minor misdemeanor. This selfishness is working against your marriage.

Being fair requires one to be humble and honest. The same advantages you give yourself are the same benefits you must give your spouse. If you can stay out with your friends, then so can they. If you get to overspend, then so can they. One thing you must understand is that they are adults just as you and your behavior inadvertently gives them the same privileges.

In other words, if you don't like it, then don't do it. If you don't like mistreatment, then don't mistreat others. It's the old statement that says, "Do unto others, as you would have them do unto you." In marriage, you must be fair enough to give your mate the same benefits, privileges, rewards, and advantages that you give yourself. If you don't, then you are too selfish to be married in the first place.

NOTES

Day 28

NAKED AND NOT ASHAMED.

By Sabrina Shaw

Everything looks beautiful with cosmetics. Ladies, we know how to beat our face, get our nails and feet done, get our hair done and put on some things. But does he know how you look without all that? Both looks are important in a marriage.

Remember men are visual creatures. What you looked like when he first met you, you have to keep up. You have to keep your body fit and your face fierce. Certainly, life and age are going to be major factors, but you can flow with it. Remember life and age are affecting him as well, but you must stay attractive. He used to compliment you all the time about how beautiful you are. That's because you kept it up. What is he saying now? Have the compliments stopped because your efforts stopped?

It is also important that he sees you without all the makeup. I know for many young ladies this is not difficult. The social culture has certainly changed when it comes to impressing our men. But seeing you without makeup is also a vital moment. He then knows that you are real and he can appreciate you for who you are. He notices the blemishes, the stretch marks, and the cellulite that we all cover up with contours. That is who you are without the cosmetic assistance.

Then when you get dolled up for him, it makes it all the more special.

You would not believe the number of women who have insecurities about themselves. Some men have never seen their wife totally naked. This is due to personal insecurity.

Insecurity will make you project your feelings on another. You don't think he thinks you look good, because internally you don't think you look good. This also goes both ways. Men have similar issues. Take a chance, and try it one night. Both of you sleep in the buff and enjoy each other. It could certainly be an esteem booster.

NOTES

Day 29

IT'S BETTER TO MARRY A PERSON THAN A POSITION!

By Jonathan Shaw

We all know the guy from high school who couldn't get a date or hook up with anyone. Every girl in the class or the whole school for that matter overlooked him. Twenty years later and he got a job as a CEO executive. He now owns his car and home. His handsome salary has allowed him to purchase the most updated wardrobe. He cleans up pretty well. Now the same guy that couldn't get a date is fighting off the women left and right. I wonder if the attraction is in him or his position?

I can't tell you how often I see this, especially in the church. Women and men have been known to be attracted to power, prestige, and position rather than a person.

A preacher seems attractive only because they are in a position of power. A woman seems interesting if she takes charge and gets things done. Unfortunately, too many people see these individuals as a goal and who they want in a mate. But I would suggest that they aren't attracted to the person, they are attracted to the position.

The danger of marrying a position rather than a person is that the person doesn't always behave according to their position. The position is what you do, not who you are. Just because a man is a preacher doesn't mean that he's a good husband… but it also doesn't mean that he isn't. It's important to judge a person on the merit of their character rather than their posture in a position.

Another problem with marrying a person according to their position is positions change. Just because one is doing something today, doesn't mean that is what they will be doing tomorrow. For example, if you marry a person for the church, you will always have to be in church to be married, which means you will never know how to function outside of the church setting. Don't look at the position, pay attention to the person!

Notes

Day 30

DADDY'S GIRL
YOU'RE A BIG GIRL NOW.

By Sabrina Shaw

How do you expect him to leave and cleave and you won't leave and cleave? It's wonderful to have a relationship with your father, but you have to give your husband full reign to lead your home. The daddy's girl syndrome can be detrimental in a marriage, just like the mommas' boy syndrome.

One big issue in marriage is the last name factor. The tradition is for the woman to change her last name to her husband's. I know some women who keep their maiden name or hyphenate it. Either way, you decide to do it, have you talked it over with your husband? What does he want? How does he feel that you still carry your father's name or your maiden name? This daddy's girl syndrome could be doing more damage than you realize.

Another challenge with the daddy's girl syndrome is, you need or want things done in your house. But let your husband do it, or let him find someone to do it. If the first thing you do is call daddy over or ask daddy what he thinks, it may be a problem with your husband. What does your husband think should be done is the question. Ok, maybe your man isn't handy, but he can learn to be. Now if you both agree that your father can fix it then fine, but don't question his manhood by not asking him first. And don't expect him to be exactly like daddy. He may have some of the characteristics of your dad, that's what attracted you to him, but he's not your father.

I already knew that whenever my husband and I bought our house, I was going to call my father. He was my hero. My father never got to see our first house, but my husband and I would reminisce about what I would have wanted my father to do. The good thing is my husband wouldn't have had a problem, but he showed me that he could do those things. And, things I never knew he could do. I've seen my husband fix things, build things and work on home projects. I always thought if I needed to, I would call my father. But my husband did it. If you give him a chance, yours could do it too.

Now, this same principle applies to the husbands with your mother. Don't make your wife jealous because you prefer your mothers cooking or way of doing things and you ignore your wife. If both of you agree, that's one thing, but make sure she's ok with it first.

You both are adults now and have a spouse.

Notes

DAY 31

USE EVERY ANNIVERSARY TO EVALUATE YOUR MARRIAGE.

By Jonathan Shaw

I'm happy to say that at the release of this book my wife and I have been married for 20 years. We have enjoyed our life together, and we look forward to spending many more years together in marital bliss. Many of the things that we wrote in this book are pearls of wisdom we've acquired during our 20-year marriage.

One of the things we practice in our marriage is an assessment of it. Just as children get a report card at the end of a semester to determine how well they are doing in school, so should a couple give each other a grade to determine how well they are doing as a mate. I always suggest the anniversary is a great time as any to make this assessment.

Usually, a wedding anniversary is a time that most couples are already in a happy mood. This will make each party more receptive to hearing things that aren't favorable. What should you discuss? Ask your spouse how you are doing as a husband/wife. Allow them to be honest and to speak their heart of truth. Try your best to not to interrupt them while they are speaking. This will allow them to convey a full thought and reveal their heart. It's a good practice to listen to understand instead of listening to respond.

A follow-up question is 'how can I improve on being a better husband/wife'? This question will allow your mate to tell you what they need and what they are looking for in a marriage. So often people gravitate to the social ideology of a wife or husband and those ideas may not work in every marriage. Being sufficient for the person you're married to is important. Knowing their needs and desires and satisfying them will make your marriage a happy one. Asking your mate how you can improve says that you are concerned about them and allows your spouse to go on record for telling you what they want. So you can never say you never heard it.

Everything that has any value must always have a time of assessment. Even when God created the heavens and the earth, the scripture says that at the end of each creation, He looked back at what He created and said it was good. Basically, God assessed what He created. A marriage is what you make it. So you must assess it and make sure it's good. Asking these questions is a great start to a healthy conversation of improving your marriage.

Notes

Conclusion

Thank you so much for reading our book of wisdom principles to help marriages. We believe that marriage rocks, and it's the Lord's desire for us to have loving, supportive, and healthy marriages.

Our "One Heart" Couples Ministry is dedicated to ministering to the whole marriage unit. We do not discriminate between husband, wife or children. We seek to discuss and heal more than just the sex life of couples. We minister in the areas that husbands and wives never discuss or have difficulty discussing. "One Heart" aims towards one mind, one thought, one vision, one passion, one unit and one covenant in the marital relationship.

We want to help every married couple enjoy marital bliss. We certainly don't know it all but are glad you've decided to read this book to get some great insight and learned wisdom from our experiences.

If you would like to reach out to us for counseling or join us at one of your "One Heart" gatherings, please visit our website at **www.crown-ministries.org**.

www.ingramcontent.com/pod-product-compliance
Lightning Source LLC
Chambersburg PA
CBHW071410290426
44108CB00014B/1760